What Do You Do in the Morning?

Seed Learning

wake up

take a shower

get dressed

eat breakfast

brush my teeth

wash my face

make my bed

brush my hair

What do you do in the morning?

I wake up.

What do you do in the morning?

I make my bed.

What do you do in the morning?

I take a shower.

What do you do in the morning?

I get dressed.

What do you do in the morning?

I eat breakfast.

What do you do in the morning?

I brush my teeth.

Let's learn about the Netherlands.

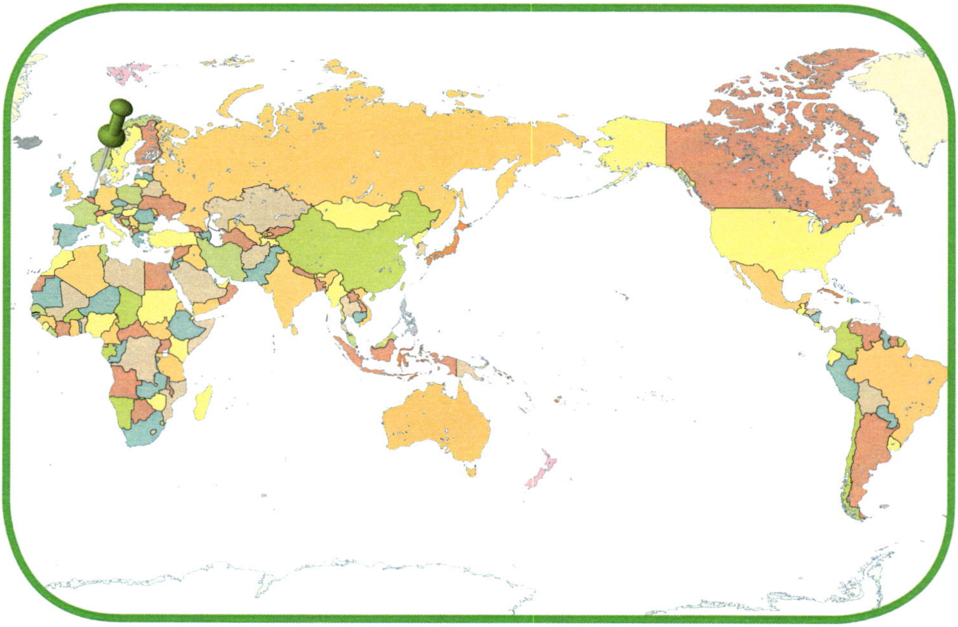

Flag of the Netherlands

Windmills